Dominic Berry is a
poet. He made his
'Lovely Fruit Salad', as an Artist in Residence at
Contact in 2007. From there, his work has taken
him to gigs in Germany, France, The Netherlands
and USA, and tours of Canada, India, New Zealand
and Australia.

His awards include winning Manchester Literature
Festival's Superheroes of Slam and New York's
Nuyorican Poetry Café Slam. In 2016 he made his
performance debut at Glastonbury Festival and
his TV appearances include BBC's *Greg & Celia's
Festivals Highlights* and Channel 4's *My Daughter
the Teenage Nudist*.

To Adrian
cheers fr me
cheers!
Dom

"There are few better voices for gay geekery than Dominic Berry. His playful cadence bursts from the pages, as does a pleasingly mature side: here's a poet who appreciates "difficult second albums" and "clunky B-sides". Expect leopards and lubrications, *Minecraft* and masturbation, and a tryst or two in a toilet. In Berry's deft hands, we are but a Sega Mega Drive joy-pad: he's thumbing our buttons and I think I like it."
Fat Roland, Bad Language

"Dominic Berry has the energy of ten people. When he speaks he puts that energy into his words, then gifts them to the audience with tenderness, ferocity and passion. He writes skillfully and for the best reason: he has things to say."
Ben Fagan, Apples & Snakes

"Dominic Berry fills every page with his unique exuberant energy, wit and insight. A word warrior for the *Mortal Kombat* generation."
Tina Sederholm, Hammer & Tongue

"Dominic Berry is an extraordinary poet with extraordinary performance skills. His work is rich in rhythm and meter and both elegant and sophisticated in its use of rhyme and form. He presents one of the most diverse poetry sets on the performance circuit - always connecting, inspiring and often provoking his audience. His material can be tender or caustic. His stage persona is comic, vulnerable and hugely likeable."
Kevin Dyer, writer & director

★ Published by Flapjack Press
• Published by Stirred Press

no tigers
dominic berry

Flapjack Press
flapjackpress.co.uk

Exploring the synergy between performance and the page

Published in 2017 by Flapjack Press
Chiffon Way, Salford, Gtr Manchester
flapjackpress.co.uk

ISBN 978-0-9955012-1-8

Cover photograph & design by Brink
paulneads.co.uk

Printed by Imprint Digital
Upton Pyne, Exeter, Devon
imprintdigital.com

Some of the poems in this collection were developed with
Arts Council England and Lottery funding

LOTTERY FUNDED

Dedicated to Josh Sanders.

Our teenage nights marching through Milford Haven yelling lines from Rocky and Iggy were where I first felt the future wouldn't be all bad for a weirdo like me.

Thank you for giving this sweet transvestite a lust for life.

Contents

size of an egg cup

Versions of these poems first appeared in the following publications:

'Collecting Rare CD Singles at School in the Mid-1990's' in *Kate Bush* [Stirred Press, 2016].

'Playing *Mortal Kombat* Guarantees You Inner Calm' in *Wizard* [Flapjack Press, 2011].

'Love Poem in *Minecraft*' in *Kevin Costner's Bottom* [Stirred Press, 2017].

'ranthambore toilet without a lock' and 'this morning' in *Monsters* [Stirred Press, 2016].

Foreword

Dominic Berry's poetry pulls at the shin of your trousers like an insistent child - it is full of joy and full of upset and it has something to say. Dominic Berry the person does nothing with your trousers unless invited. His poems are tender and silly and intense, and to see them performed live is to experience a blast of energy that's a strange delight to behold and impossible to second-guess. I've seen Dom:

- Stand on a chair, hollering, microphoneless, evangelically extolling rimming
- Lie onstage cycling his high-heeled feet in the air while delivering an erotic monologue in character as Slimer from *Ghostbusters*
- Recite poems about bigotry and violence with such quiet intensity that it feels like the room will ignite
- Get near-nude in a boiling basement venue and describe fucking Blanka from *Street Fighter*.

Watching Dominic Berry read poems out loud is an *event*.

I first met Dom when he was, excluding performers, the only audience member at an event I was hosting - the first ever FLIM NITE, a now-monthly live lit cabaret I co-run with Jasmine Chatfield. I didn't know who he was, and was frankly surprised that we'd managed to get an audience member. Afterwards Jasmine told me that he was a stalwart of the Manchester poetry scene and all-around Big Deal - the kind of poet so successful it's surely only a matter of days before he has his poetry transcribed onto the side of an abandoned pub. We met properly, I grovelled, and he rewarded my unhealthy begging by performing at our *Terminator 2*-themed event with a new poem. It was empathetic and powerful and I felt very cool for having prompted it, despite being in no way responsible for any of the empathetic powerful stuff in it. It's in this book, about which I feel unjustifiably proud. It is, like a lot of Dom's work, a poem to make you feel better, and a poem to make you be better.

The uncompromising intensity of his live stuff loses nothing on the page. You are about to read stories of brutality and heartache and queer pride and vegan pride and love love love in the face of overwhelming injustice. Some laugh in the faces of those who would hurt us and some comfort those who are hurting. The beating heart of these poems is kindness, and it is a kindness that says *things are not as they should be, sometimes everything is sore, this is how we should try and make it better*.

Jack Nicholls

19th Century Boy

"I like my work and do as I am told.
For every carpet colour, there's a dye.
The brilliant blue is shining, bright as gold.

I am a draw boy. I am twelve years old.
I follow Father with my head held high.
I like my work and do as I am told.

As Father fights a drunk man in the cold
outside the pub, I stare up at the sky.
The brilliant blue is shining, bright as gold.

At Sunday School, the teachers scowl and scold.
I pray to God and wait for a reply.
I like my work and do as I am told.

Bring Mother money from each carpet sold.
Ten pence a yard. I look her in the eye.
The brilliant blue is shining, bright as gold.

I'm working. I don't need a hand to hold.
I hear my Father shout, my Mother cry.
I like my work and do as I am told.
The brilliant blue is shining, bright as gold."

hardworking families

On 6th November 1966, Scottish pop singer Lulu released 'I'm a Tiger'. It reached number 9 in the UK singles chart and stayed in the Top 75 for 13 weeks. Like most of her 1960s' recordings, Lulu no longer performs the song, and now regularly speaks negatively about it in interviews. Near the end of the song, Lulu growls whilst pronouncing the r of 'tiger'. In the 1980s, Lulu was a vocal supporter of Thatcher.

Lulu is no tiger.

On 25th June 1993, Midway released the violent video game *Mortal Kombat 2*. The game features a four-armed monster by the name of Kintaro. Midway initially planned for Kintaro to be a two-armed half-human half-tiger, but early designs were scrapped when the programmers were unable to create an appearance of fur with which everyone was happy.

Kintaro is no tiger.

On 29th March 2016, I joined the gay sex app Grindr.

At its best, Grindr is a forum for confident fellows to share flattering photographs of their splendid genitalia.

At its worst, Grindr is a little bit Nazi.

"NO ASIANS"
"NO BLACKS"
"NO CHUBBY FEMMES"

In the UK, we have had the legalisation of gay marriage and the increasing acceptance of a certain kind of homosexual into the British mainstream. There are many men who have sex with men who don't give a flying fuck about the vulnerable and oppressed because they now have a mortgage, have never felt discrimination, and own more feta cheese than any middle-class chap could ever find use for.

I am a 37-year-old versatile top, looking for furry guys with stripes who know how to growl and are up for a fight.

Final Boss

There is a guy who likes to fight
inside his tiny flat.
His thumbs are drumming death-moves on
a black controller pad.
Today, he'll top his highest score.
He feels it in his heart.
He sits beside his PS4.
He presses ⊗. It starts.

He knows he won't be going out.
The people talk and stare.
Down at the shop, his breath would stop.
He'd start to gasp for air.
No air. He'd fall. No air. They'd call
him names. His shame. His sweat.
How can he master life's controls?
He can't control his breath.

What if the children spat at him?
What if some stones were thrown?
What if a girl began to laugh
and filmed it on her phone?
What if a normal woman,
in her normal coat and hat,
thought she could say, "Are you OK?"
He couldn't cope with that.

There is no cheat to beat this game,
achievements will stay locked,
but in his flat he's got some soup
and half a can of pop,
so here, at home, he's saved. Alone.
He knows he won't be ill.
His PS4 says *Level Up*.
He presses ⊗ to kill.

Perch

You hover above the lone insomniac.
Silent crow in her ear.

She tried to close the window earlier
but that won't always stop you getting in.

Deafening stillness.
Fatter every visit.

You start as no more than an image of wings.
Tells herself it's only feathers until

      beak

             pecks

                     unpick

                           eyelids.

Scrunched raw under duvet,
her shoulders are in the wrong places
and there are so many dreams she wants to dream
but can't even get lying right.
Dreams might be best left for the dead.

She once thought her head was solid, but it is not.
Your talons pass through her skull
as simply as a bird scooping fish from water.
Big wishes in a tiny pond.

Take it.
Take it all from her head.
Take the tears she talked about crying but didn't,
the faces of people she was too tangled to kiss,
the throat lumps,
scoop them out.
Rip.
Is she too sweaty to ever be hugged?
Should she spend more money?
Better deodorant?
Impressive perfume?
Do some hugs cost more than others?
If she accepts that,
might she finally be able to afford a dream?
Dreams might be best left for the dead.

Swallow.
Regurgitate.
Swallow.
Regurgitate.
Take
and take until

minutes before her morning alarm,
only then do you choose to fly away.

A Poem Spoken by Sarah Connor from *Terminator 2*

"Show me a man who knows
there is nothing wrong with eyes that cry.
A crying man is not breaking down.
A man who can block his tears is not fixed.
Eyes are valves,
not sealed circuits closed shut.
Only open eyes can see.

Show me a man who knows how to see,
who will stay with my child
and me.

Show me a man who will hear my son's howls
and know
they are the sound of his engine accelerating.
This internal combustion marks the start of a path
to all that his pain and love will generate.
Show me a man who will help me raise him,
who won't shut him down,
who knows why we cry
or at least
show me a man I can teach.

I am teaching my child
tears can repair.
When he sees the damage done he will care
and want to try to mend.

I am teaching my child
it's not too much for a man
to try
to be human."

Hardworking Families

You'll never clean toilets for cash.
You're someone who'll never need charity.
You'll never get spots or a rash
for you're in a hardworking family.

You'll never get cramp or chlamydia.
You are an icon of normality.
Your child can't have spina bifida
for you're in a hardworking family.

You'll never need badgers or foxes.
Your healthcare is just a formality.
You'll never sleep in cardboard boxes
for you're in a hardworking family.

A loved one cannot tell you lies.
Your grandma will not lose her sanity.
You're safe while the sea levels rise
for you're in a hardworking family.

The Tories will cleanse all the mess
when rioting leads to fatality.
You'll never get mugged or depressed
for you're in a hardworking family.

You won't break your arm, or a sweat,
or face any kind of calamity.

You'll feel no harm, or regret,
for you're in a hardworking family.

Another Cut

and Kate's new jeans have got a tear.
She cut the tag the shop put there.
She heard they'd doubled the bus fare
while she was cutting her son's hair.
A nurse was kind to Kate back when
her mind and skin were not best friends.
She cuts the mould from off the bread
then thinks of cuts that she can't mend.

Another cut.
Another cut

A suited man on a great lake
will claim that this is the best place
for his dad's yacht when he must take
the time to find which cuts he'll make.
He cuts with fingers scalpel thin
to keep the budget neatly trimmed.
While someone cuts his sandwiches
he gets a man to shave his chin.

Another cut.
Another cut.

The more that man can cut and cut
our hospitals, our schools, our art,
our shelters and our youth clubs shut,
the more of us start to cut.

We cut our arms. We cut our legs.
We cut our wrists and backs of heads.
The poorest skin now sunbed red.
Another cut. Another dead.

Another cut.
Another cut

and Kate cuts
another cut.

Men Locked Behind Toilet Doors

Jack and Ben are men locked behind a toilet door. Jack is fucking Ben's arse. The air is hot and smells of vomit. Ben knows Jack owns every Bjork CD even the remix ones yes even the shit remix ones. Ben's shit is on Jack's legs and inside Jack's boxer shorts. Ben thinks, *Don't stop*. Never. Be. Lonely. The sound of half a phone call is heard outside. Another man explains to someone else that he needs it Thursday not Friday *no it has to be Thursday no listen it must be Thursday no you don't understand Thursday Thursday fuck*. Ben thinks, *Don't stop*. Great pain. Jack does not know Ben's name. Jack adores the taste of his own sweat *mmm yes* he licks his upper lip *mmm yes* he wishes someone was filming him right now xtube this is love *mmm yes* this could go viral.

Tom is alone. Locked behind a toilet door. It is nine days until Tom's 14th birthday. The air smells of bleach. Never. Be. Lonely. *Thump* someone's boot kicks the outside of the toilet door *come out queer fucking queer I'm going to get you fucking queer fucking queer fuck you queer fuck you*. Tom does not know if he is gay. Tom knows this is fear. Will never leave. He will die.

Thump Tom knows that there will never be a day when he won't be a man locked behind some toilet door *come out fucking queer*. Tom. Can't. Cry.

William is locked behind a toilet door. They made him play as the fat guy in *Mortal Kombat X*. No one likes the fat guy in *Mortal Kombat X*. He wants to be a Thunder God. Would settle for a ninja but they made him play as the fat guy in *Mortal Kombat X*. Fat guy spits fat balls of puke. *Use fingers* William. *Special moves* William. Quarter circle down throat down down left right purge. William no longer chokes on chunks will often use his toothbrush today it's only fingers it's almost like thin lightning bolts splat pattern porcelain. Milkshake. Waffles. Scrambled egg. *Splat splat splat.* One day he will be God of Thunder. Never. Be. Lonely and don't tell mum and don't tell mum and don't tell mum and don't tell mum and don't tell mum.

Dan is a man locked behind a toilet door. Yes. Cocaine-caked nostrils. Yes. Dan's atoms are sexy dancing high kicks. Yes. Dan's mum wouldn't know a sexy atom not if she saw one do the splits. Dan's friend outside, *I'll be ok in a minute mate, I'll be ok in a minute mate* fuck off mate Dan's atoms are vibrating exploding shaking their groove thang what kind of lame arse atoms do you have anyway mate there are disco atoms in Dan's dick and there are disco atoms in Dan's fist and there are tingly sharp atoms in Dan's disco nose. Never. Be. Lonely. Dan knows

it is not on top of Tibetan mountains. Nirvana is here. Dan has never heard a remix album by Bjork. Dan unlocks his toilet door. Steps outside and Dan. Can. Breathe. Fuck. Dan. Can. Breathe.

Collecting Rare CD Singles at School in the Mid-1990s

Joanne has many loud and busy friends
but she does not have 'Alchemy'.
'Alchemy' is a B-side
on the 1994 Kate Bush CD single, 'Red Shoes'.

Miranda Richardson was in the video.
Her hands were hurt and bandaged.

'Alchemy' is not on CD2 of the 2 CD set.
Only CD1.
It is rare.
Difficult to own.

One copy can be found in a dark, indoor market,
June 1996, in London's Covent Gardens,
lodged between albums by Pet Shop Boys
and
Kiki Dee,
next to the jewellery stall that smells of pizza,
255 miles from Joanne's school.
You would have to search to find it.
The person who sells these CDs speaks as if
he doesn't realise their worth.

'Alchemy' is a quiet, slow song about a man.

No friends.
Only bees.
Imagine believing you own bees.

Joanne doesn't know who Kate Bush is.
No one in this school knows what bees are worth
and the songs they own are all in the Top Ten.

The peak position of Kate Bush's 'Red Shoes'
in the official UK Singles Chart is 21.
It is not a song many people want to have.

Maybe no one at Joanne's school has 'Alchemy'.
The children here are loud, busy and speak as if
they don't realise their worth.

you don't have to take your clothes off

I know what you're thinking. This poetry is all well and good but when can we see Dominic Berry's penis?

Well, it's funny you should bring that up. Early in my career, I was invited to recite my words for a group of nudists. I was told by the organisers that everyone in my audience would be naked, but they added,

> "You don't have to take your clothes off, Dominic."
> *You* don't have to take your clothes off, Dominic.
> You don't *have* to take your clothes off, Dominic.

Well, when in Rome…

I was then told that the event was being filmed for a television documentary.

It'll stun you to learn not all of us poets are millionaires. Often, when we are invited to perform at a gig that isn't the best paid work, organisers will try to entice us with talk of "Sky Arts might be there" … and Sky Arts are *never* there.

However, at this event, a film crew *was* there, and as I lowered my underpants in front of the Channel 4 cameras, I thought, *Could this be a mistake?*

Well, the programme had the not-at-all creepy title *My Daughter the Teenage Nudist.* Lovely name.

I am not going to show you my penis within the pages of this book. However, it is on 4OD. I encourage you all to enjoy my penis in the comfort of your own homes as many times as you desire.

My penis is nothing if not easily accessible.

My Rude Elbow

My elbow is so sexy it could detonate a church.
A picture of me shirtless is like a Greek God.

Just a peak of this elbow's raw flesh
and married men's vows of fidelity
will be forgotten.
Trousers will drop to ankles
and the united seismic force
of their violent, public masturbation
will threaten to rip apart Britain's economy,
overthrow the monarchy
and release total orgiastic anarchy.

Your grandmother once saw me expose myself.
She had to pretend she was appalled,
but I know that one fleeting sight
of my nude elbow
gave your nan her first multiple orgasm.
She said she hadn't felt that alive since the war.

International terrorists have an iPhone app.
A close up pic of this elbow can be sent
to any screen anywhere in the world.
If you see my elbow *that* close, *that* naked,
both your eyes turn inside out.
Squelch! Squelch!
Elbow porn murder.

I never asked to have elbows this erotic.

No wonder
some only share theirs behind locked doors.

Picture this:
your elbow. My tongue.
Everyone watching.
Slobber. Slurp. Lick.
Everyone, rolling up sleeves.
Everyone, bare arm joint on bare arm joint.
Every gender, creed and age;
indiscriminate, unleashed, undeniable.
No longer locked under shirt,
understand,
we're unstoppable.

Join me!

We will change the world.
How could we not?

No one will laugh
or make fun of your elbow
because our elbows
are fucking hot.

You are Welcome to the Family

Players on *The Dad Show*,
please welcome... Dad.
Fingers on your buffet.
Let the silence begin.

Can you hold your tongue while Dad's cousin
panic attacks all over the hummus?
She's lost it.
Dad is judging the score lines on her wrist.
He drops more N bombs
than vine leaves have rice.

Keep your mouth shut as Mum pretends
it's only chopped onions that make her cry.
What are women like? Don't answer.
The correct response is smile.
Dad blames The Immigrants
for all he never did.

Repress for success.
Your anger is never right.

Win Dad's approval and you might get
invited to the summer BBQ, a holiday or two,
where everyone will wear lovely smiles
full of silence.
Dreams of what will be left when he's gone.

Imagine if you walked away empty handed.

Playing *Mortal Kombat* Guarantees You Inner Calm

This is an age of caged hostility
where Health & Safety forms and files
fry brains, pry pains,
our supposed source of security sees highs waned
and lives drained.
Cries contained can't scream through offices,
rip through orifices,
or express a desk job's bubbling
hate, hurt and harm

but playing *Mortal Kombat*
guarantees you inner calm.
Maybe play as Jax.
Tear off someone's arm.
Perform an 'Organ Donor'.
Crush a heart inside your palm.
Playing *Mortal Kombat*
guarantees you inner calm.

Insurance claims and tax returns
incite most deadly vows
but Sonya Blade's leg toss
can never fail to arouse.
Funding forms leave hair-lines torn.
Make us curse and hiss.
Sub Zero's spine-cord rip will induce
instant love and bliss.

Baraka's blades decapitate
with almost cheeky charm.
Playing *Mortal Kombat*
guarantees you inner calm.

Without *Mortal Kombat*
I'd have murdered half my school
and every boss I've ever had.
Fatality by duel.
But *Mortal Kombat* soothed my wrath.
I felt my fury fade.
Let us respect its full effect
with a worldwide parade!

Let's sing of Queen Sindel in hymns.
Perhaps we'll pen a psalm.
>   *Playing Mortal Kombat*
>   *Guarantees...*
If life's been hard, left you scarred,
here's a healing balm.
Playing *Mortal Kombat*
guarantees you inner calm.

Love Poem in *Minecraft*

I want to love you but not in this world.
Want our lives to entangle and plans to unfurl
away from a space where normality's hurled
in our faces and we're told our place.

I am too weird for this world. We need *Minecraft*.
Build our own thrills. Fulfil what we might have
if we're allowed to be proud when we find daft
delights in the sprites we embrace.

Laugh at my pixeled eyes or my square feet.
Open my chest. Take this heart. Will you meet
on the map I made for you? It's only complete
when you're here. I think you're ace.

I think you're ace. You are the greatest.
Don't turn off my game or put my life on stasis.
These mountains and caves I made are the basis
of somewhere for you to see me.

If you'll see me, I will build all your dreams.
Make a forest of cake full of fizzy pop streams.
Have my last potion. You know what that means.
I'm whoever you want me to be.

With the best armour, I'll save you from trouble.
Dig for your gold. Hand me that shovel.

I can be Alex if you hate Steve's stubble.
Whatever you want, I'll agree

if you don't ever leave. I know I am strange
but whatever you don't like about me I'll change.
In this block world of *Minecraft* we can rearrange
anything you don't like. Stay.

I will build a new face if you'll stay in this game,
build a new world if you think my map's lame,
whatever you like I will just like the same.
If you give the command, I'll obey.

My love keeps shining like diamonds of blue.
In a land full of lies, will my made-up one do?
Let's invent our reality. Make it come true.
Promise you won't go away.

Time Travelled

You tell me again
the years I remember never existed.

There is a photo of us
in a place where we have never been,
fading like the family in *Back to the Future*.
I have imagined whole albums of memories
which will now never exist.
You. Me. Together. Old.
A sci-fi epic love where these heroes never die.
These heroes never lived.

Two people can be in the same room,
same moment
and still be in completely different places.

This doesn't feel like Time travelling.
This feels like being Time's hostage.
Time's gun against my head,
promising to blow to bits everything I am
desperate
to keep.

Time keeps driving forward.
Racing anger gets me nowhere.

Time is powerful;

too often slams its foot on the pedal
to speed through the best bits,
and then slows down to first gear
to cruise the scenic route
of every aching country mile
of heartbreak.

"Wake up."

Time whacks the butt of its revolver
against my head
and I have the shocking realisation that I am not
supreme controller of every event in the universe.

I was never a Time Lord.

Time travels.
Destination: irrelevant.

You tell me again
the years I remember never existed

and all I have is this journey.

You Are Good at Silence

Your silence does not flinch.
It's not weighted with jagged, awkward angles.
No heavy expectations.
Your silence is light and strong.
What a skill to listen so steadily.
What a skill to leave my tears unsteered
and keep your silence this calm.
Hot water bottle on a stormy night.
I think I just dribbled on your jumper.
Your silence is never phased by drool.
Your silence is not dry-clean only.
It welcomes whatever is thrown against it
with hugs.
Solid enough to let sadness be.

You are also good at not being silent.
Fashioning the loudest laughter into
a one voice choir of harmonic chaos
and wit quicker than time can catch.
An hour's laughter with you feels like minutes.
You are more powerful than Time,
wielding your words with flare and
fabulous ferocity.
This time in your silence makes me
value our cacophonous times all the more.

I'm not always good at silence.

Too many words jumping in my throat.
Thoughts too bouncy.
I'm often more Tigger than Winnie the Pooh.
Silence can look like a bear.
Hairy mass that blocks the sun.

You show me that doesn't have to be true.

True silence is kind.
Confident.
Just there.

I want to learn to be silent
like you.

I Will Not Treat a Friend Like an iPod

An iPod is a thing which is made to break,
to use until it doesn't work for you
and then throw away,
knowing your money will get you a better one,
the latest one, ready for temporary adoration.

I will not be told that a friend with depression
should be thrown away

or that a happy person
is a better person.

You can sing me all your tracks.
Not just the cheesy pop
which you think will make me smile.

Give me your difficult second album,
the one with all the distorted, guitar feedback
and seven minute jazz piano solos.

Sometimes,
what many dismiss as an obscure, clunky B-side
can give deeper meanings that last
and are far too precious
to delete from any library.

An iPod is made to break,
but Leonard Cohen sang,

"There is a crack in everything.
That's how the light gets in."

You are my Leonard Cohen.
You are my Justin Bieber.

We are weird, wailing
Kate Bush, 'Waking the Witch'.
We are live, bootleg,
Marvin Gaye's final concert, 1983.
I believe we can always be
Chemical Brothers.
Scissor Sisters.
Sister Sledge.
'We are Family'.
I believe we will always be.

An iPod is made to break.
All of us are built to sing.

Pub Triolet

Awash with cheer, my flood of friends,
whose words are wet with wit and glee,
share juice and beer. Your laughter mends,
awash with cheer. My flood of friends,
I'll join you here, for this time sends
my sorrow somewhere far from me.
Awash with cheer, my flood of friends,
whose words are wet with wit and glee.

bigger cats

On 3rd May 2016, I was given work reciting poems in North India. The bones of a dead stag lay outside the door of the place where for several weeks I would be sleeping. I was told, "A leopard killed that."

My first night there I told my hosts I was going out for an evening walk. "Aren't you worried about leopards?" they asked. I stayed in.

On 2nd July 2009, the Delhi High Court made a move towards legalising homosexuality in India.

On 11th December 2013, the Supreme Court of India overturned their ruling. Indian gays are currently living illegally.

I spent much of my time in India with children and their families performing my silly poems about monsters and magic. I was told many of these young people had never learnt how to play.

No one there would ever call me gay. Too big an insult.

Everyone I encountered was well educated on environmental matters, many ate vegan diets, and all were dedicated to the preservation of the natural habitat of the endangered tigers which I was informed, if I was lucky, I might get the chance to see.

date in delhi

many queers here do not put their faces on grindr
sometimes they use superheroes
batman scowls
black widow winks

some use pictures of open mouthed tigers
bare teeth
longing tongues
often the image is blank

several lizards are panicking up my hotel wall
one is trying to hide behind the long strip-light
but I see narrow fingers of a statuesque hand
jut out like points of a cartoon explosion

street police have big guns and bigger smiles
it is a good morning sir

i meet mike our coffee mugs look like egg cups
mike has bold muscles shares his confident belief
india will treat its gays like england does now
within the next three years
between swallowed shots of scalding latte

i am told to walk carefully
mosquitoes and homophobes are everywhere

i am told to eat carefully
but the confident flow of my fiery diarrhoea
has long since taken its residence
in this delicate stomach
relentless with its stinging certainty

it doesnt feel like this is ever going to change

the track to sawai madhopur

long limbed man clambers into luggage rack
drops his head on my bag
smiles and snores
seats full of men perched on other mens knees
laugh on this thirteen hour train journey
sometimes the air conditioning works
merry men talk and i dont understand

a stranger opposite removing his shoes
places his bare feet on my legs
the new prodigy is on my ipod shuffle

there is no glass in my window
outside hundreds of men in fields
shit
bent kneed squatting flat feet on ground
wide eyes watching me watching them
penises and testicles dangle
dry heat and cracked mud
communities come together
shit
and watch me pass

i am later told that the buckets i see contain
river water they
shit
wash hands

empty the bucket
and take it away
milk the cow
somewhere i wont see

ranthambore toilet without a lock

bones of a recently killed stag
mauled by leopards lie outside my room
locals tease my queasy hunt
across the forest for toilet tissue

after three days i discover a way
you can make this toilet spray
clean water up your butt
feel rimmed by a dozen loving tongues

after nine days i discover
different settings on that spray
twelve tongues a hundred tongues
a thousand tongue rockets

this morning

an old man went out alone
and met a leopard who smashed down
the wall by our stream
lucky to still be here

locked in a jeep i am driven by that stream
strewn with broken brick close eyes
picture
guts torn out in the water

stomach wrench teeth clench
the driver is asking do i have a wife
broken brains blood bones
guts torn out in the water

instructions for meeting a leopard alone

stand motionless
leopards hate sudden movements
like fleeing for your life or jazz hands

jazz hands are everything to a performance poet
far more important than any of the words
leopards see spoken word art as an attack

impressive tales of sexual prowess wont shield
cassanova credentials
cant stop crunching bone

welcome to the family

the deer and monkeys raid the trash
they find behind the boarding school
in burnt out fires charcoal ash
the suns so bright the sky is full

arbaz has carefully cut out
a drawing from his toothpaste case
a dragon who can soar and shout
is saved from joining kitchen waste

his friend arpit and he collect
the pictures offered by colgate
a king a castle quite a set
the heroes spar until its late

they share a dorm with thirty boys
and dream of witches flying by
to fight with knights their cardboard toys
have swords so sharp they slash the sky

arbaz will share the games theyve played
what these two travellers have won
they never seem to be afraid
their joy is bigger than the sun

no tiger

through great safari gates our jeeps drive
like jurassic world
except fewer dinosaurs
maybe tigers
not genetically modified tree frog t-rex tigers
tigers are cool enough

5am in rajasthan is cool enough to compare to
an impressive british summer day
amber sunrise
no tiger

we see prancing peacocks with fat tails
mother monkeys breastfeed babies
white spotted chital deer
approach each jeep
tiny water spots on noses
apologies for todays lack of violence
apologies for not getting eaten

what if there are no tigers
are they added to films post production
are the movies all cgi effects
is this tiger myth a money making scam
are tigers already extinct

here are the herbivores
nothing more

hear john williams
famous score
before
people ruin things

opening credits
close up
lake
ripple

Tiger

We chat of cats in cramped safari jeeps.
Politely by the lake, we watch the deer.
We gave our time expecting more than this.
The tigers we had hoped to find aren't here.
Then, in a blink, the deer leap up and flee.
The landscape's cleared by flurried fear's alarm
and all at once the air is bathed in hope.
Elated thrill soaks any sense of calm.

We grab at phones. Somebody shouts and points.
The guide enforces quiet, then we drive
towards a distant dot, which now we know
is what we were all hoping would arrive.
A tiger strides, without a growl or snarl.
His massive muscles move him over sand.
Those claws could tear my foot off in a flash.
The guide is pointing with an outstretched hand.

No cage between this jeep and all those teeth.
The silent, open mouth that long tongue licks
could easily crack through my skull, my spine,
as everyone's extending selfie sticks.
I sit and watch the tiger turn away.
We grabbed our prizes. Snaps to feed our greed.
We paid our time. We were not killed today.
We leave with more than any of us need.

size of an egg cup

In the Sega Mega Drive video game *Terminator 2*, you could only be Terminator.

I didn't want to be Terminator.

I wanted to be the mum.

The Conservative government of my youth called single mums 'spongers'.

A dangerous drain on our welfare state.

When I saw single mum Sarah Connor in *Terminator 2*, I didn't see a sponger.

I saw a fighter.

I saw a teacher.

Panic is Not the Size of an Egg Cup

If there are times when your body feels
the size of an egg cup,
but the anxiety in you is bigger than an ostrich,
then it is impossible to keep that much panic in.
Forgive yourself.

The thought of exploding
in front of some stranger
swells that dread.
Forgive yourself.

Strangers say strange things.
That's what make them strangers.

If words blade against your balloon brain
until something must burst
it is better
to stay in bed

bandaged
in
duvet.

Sadness is Not the Size of an Egg Cup

If there are times when your body feels
the size of an egg cup,
but the sadness inside you is desert-wide,
you will cry tears dry.

It is impossible to keep that much sadness in.
Waterless trails claw cheeks like cactus spikes.
Burning Sun God talons
turn clock face to hieroglyphs

but you know these times of sadness cannot last,
like an egg timer knows the back of its sand.
If you can embrace that pain and let it flow
you can create a space where happiness will grow.

Happiness is Not the Size of an Egg Cup

If there are times when your body feels
the size of an egg cup,
but the joy inside you is the size of a shooting star,
it is impossible to keep that much light in.

You have earned this time.
Let happiness shine.

There are those who will try
to use their power to dim.
If your happiness can piss those people off
then you are doing something right.

There are some colours so bright
only the sparkiest can see them.

Shine bright enough for those who know
fevered, shadowed insanities of sorrow
to find and share your light.

Even though you are only an egg cup
you can hold a shooting star.
You could catch a falling star.
Could you hatch a breaking egg?

When you have broken and exploded before,
you have always pieced yourself together.

This world makes too many Humpty Dumptys
teetering on the edge of their own existence.
Some people break
and can't be put back together by you

but if you can catch
a person's shell as they fall
you have done the best thing
any egg cup can do.

Beleaguered Vegan

This vegan is beleaguered.
All this green cuisine tastes great,
but every time he's out there's someone
studying his plate;
a person who will grill him on
his strange new-age ambition.
It seems so many meat eaters
have doctorates in nutrition.

"What you eating? Clumps of grass?"
he's asked about his platter.
"You need to eat the meat of beasts,
just don't eat those that matter.
No cats. No dogs. Try beef. This steak
is cruelty free… I'm told
and why would those who want my money
lie about what's sold?

It's normal. I'm not being rude
but I can't eat your vegan food
like… apples. I enjoy a treat
and fruit is all you vegans eat.
Such little choice, I have no doubt,
I know I couldn't live without
my donuts, custard, burgers, noodles
chocolates, chillis, apple strudels,

macaroni, strawberry shakes,
falafel, pizzas, curries, cakes,
there's so much food I know I'd miss.
A shame you can't have none of this.
I love it here. This food's the best.
What's that…? It's… vegan…? Yeah… I guessed.
You've just confirmed what I had feared.
I knew this meal tasted weird."

This vegan is beleaguered,
but before his vegan days
he once called vegans crazy,
thought their lifestyles 'just a phase'
and claimed his meat died happy,
but was he there when she died?
Should we trust some unseen farm
and never look inside

when we could listen to Thom Yorke
and vegans who inspire:
Alicia Silverstone.
Benjamin Zephaniah.
Pretenders' Chrissie Hynde.
Jackass's Steve O.
Def Jam's Russell Simmons.
This vegan's come to know

the way these days our milk is made.
It's hardly 'happy' how
a constant chain of pregnancies
are forced upon each cow.

We hear of free range chicken hens,
not what a cockerel's worth.
On free range farms they still grind up
the male chicks at birth.

So, share the films of animals
we're told are done no harm
and battle global warming,
stop the gas from modern farms,
and seek out other vegans,
for in numbers, there is might.
No time to be beleaguered.
It is time to join the fight.

Cheap Vegan

Is a vegan life a big commitment?
What's the cost? What are the limitations?
Trust your tongue. Try oral explorations.
In my kitchen there's no big equipment
but I know my beans are not deficient.
My dips are such saucy stimulations.
Boiling pulses' creamy lubrications
give an easily supplied fulfilment.

Hot or raw, my vegan led lifestyle
fills us both because I'm versatile.
Next time, try my oven for yourself.
Slide your roast into my bottom shelf.
Where the vegan party never ends
it can stretch to fit in all your friends.

Definition of Success

Not good enough to feel bad.
Not rich enough to earn poor health.
No privilege of being mad
with fortunes of good mental wealth.

Decided when each life's begun;
who'll lose their minds, who'll lose their homes,
who'll starve to death, who'll die too young,
whose brains will break, who'll die alone.

From palace grounds to terrace towns,
whose life's worth more? Whose life's worth less
when judging life in pence and pounds?
A definition of success.

I Hope This Poem Makes Me Lots of Money

The Headline Poet strides off stage to rapturous applause having been paid for his twenty minute spoken word set what it would take me a month to earn and I am not jealous. The Headline Poet is excellent at getting Headline Poetry gigs he can run a workshop balance a budget is even invited to meetings and that is the same as writing good poetry. The Headline Poet has spent twenty minutes shouting about how delicate he is detailing his history of receiving abuse and funding his pain fists beatings bruises and he has told us to check our privilege check your fucking privilege you congregation of moronic arse-wipes and buy my book.

He lets me share his taxi to a sterile hotel and shows me how to yell at an immigrant taxi driver when he won't break the law by parking in an illegal space I mean for fuck's sake we write haiku. He lets me share a table at a restaurant and shows me how to loudly humiliate a minimum waged waiter who wasn't quick enough delivering our curly fries this is cold shout at that idiot make him blush make him piss his prissy Primark pants call him girl weak little girl we got cold curly fries.

One day I will kill the Headline Poet. One day I will write a poem so heartfelt so humble and so very fucking brave that all the Headline Poets bookings will start to go to me after all isn't that the purpose of us spending all this time together. One day I will have the chance to share a poem so enlightening it will become the new dictionary definition of socialism. I don't care how many ignorant talentless open mic cunts I need to stamp on so that my kind poem can be heard. One day funders will pay me for my kind words what it would take you a year to earn and you will thank me for it while the Headline Poet lies forgotten decomposing beneath a tomb of perfectly completed evaluation forms.

I will not be lonely no one has told me if this will feel lonely but it can't be lonely right you do like me right didn't you hear my poem you must agree my poem is kind.

so get out your smartphone and open 'APPY APP™ because we all have smartphones. Don't worry about what you'll do just open 'APPY APP™ on your walk home and everything nasty: filtered.

A homeless woman being kicked in the head? Filtered: becomes Theresa May dressed as Mother Christmas singing red fur white snow blue blooded songs of Brexit and God. Maybe she'll do that nice Kate Bush one about running. There are no hills with 'APPY APP™. There is no rape no racism no litter for you to see. Everything nasty: filtered. Dog shit becomes Moses-like stone tablets foretelling low interest rates. A passing lorry packed with pre-slaughter pigs transforms into a princess-saving superguy with matching merch and jolly jokes about silly men in tights. Almost as funny as that *Mrs Brown's Boys* and we got a whole channel now that shows nothing but that on repeat forever.

Home. With 'APPY APP™ you can compare happiness scores with friends. Emily was happy 293 times this week. You only registered 261 times. Fuck. A homeless woman being kicked in the head? Imagine what that sad sight would do to Emily's happiness score. Send it in a sticker send it in a GIF spread it on Emily's wall. Break her filter. Flawless victory.

Outside. Shouting. Sirens. Smashing. Cheering. Calling. Kicking. Singing.

Inside. Do you remember when everyone had *Pokemon Go* and the NHS? There is no God but you have bought the app that sucks your fat shaves body hair pumps biceps debits your bank while you sleep. It's all about big guns. For only 59.99 a week have 'APPY APP™ wirelessly linked to your genitals electronically stimulated orgasm like *Star Trek* said we all have holodecks so who needs real sex? Feeling costs more.

A homeless woman being kicked in the head? Just another meme on the screen as you lie in your chosen franchise of paradise block all calls set wallpaper do not disturb this is bliss. Objectively prove you are safe and secured.

Terms and conditions apply.